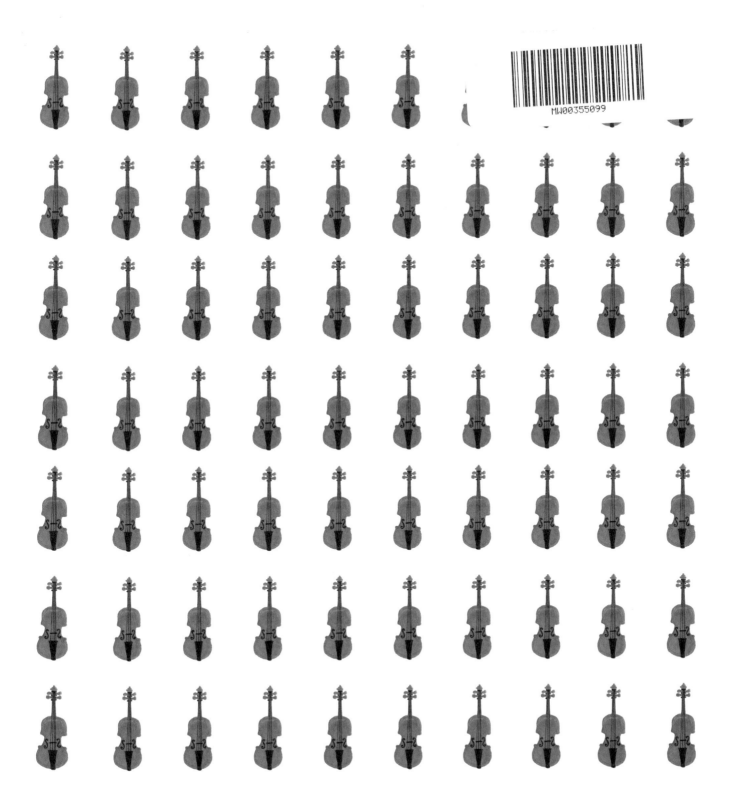

For my vibrant mother-in-law, Vittoria,
who is very valuable to me.

What does Victoria see in the mirror?
A vase, vegetables or a violin?

What does Victoria see in the mirror?
Vegetables, a volleyball or a violin?

What does Victoria see in the mirror?
A violet, a van or a violin?

What does Victoria see in the mirror?
A vacuum, a van or a violin?

What does Victoria see in the mirror?
A Valentine, a vegetable or a vest?

What does Victoria see in the mirror?
A vase, a volcano or a violin?

What does Victoria see in the mirror?
A Valentine, a violet or a volleyball?

What does Victoria see in the mirror?
A vase, vegetables or a violin?

What does Victoria see in the mirror?
A violin, Valentine, or violets?

What does Victoria see in the mirror?
A Valentine, a volcano or a violin?

Now Victoria can go in her van
with her violin, to Venice for her
Valentine concert!

V
words

vegetables

I LOVE YOU!

Valentine

vest

violin

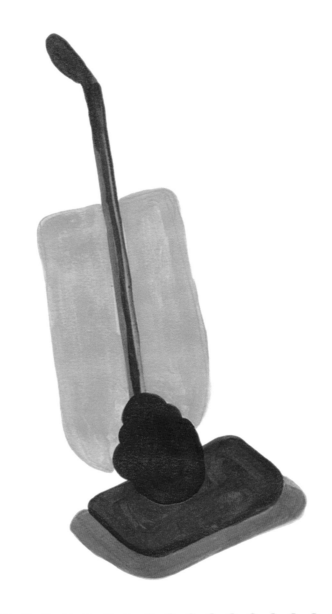

vacuum

volleyball

vase

vesuvius

volcano

violets

van

V is for Venus Effect

When the person in the artwork is looking into a mirror at the artist, not at themselves!

Some famous artists that used the Venus Effect in their artwork were Vasari and Velàzquez.

V is for Venus Effect

Make your own
VENUS EFFECT ART!

Draw yourself looking into a mirror. Your reflection should be looking back at you, the artist.

AlphaBOX Book Series

APPLES AND APRICOTS
by H.P. Gentileschi
A

Boy on a Bus
by H.P. Gentileschi
B

Cat in a Cup
by H.P. Gentileschi
C

Duck's Days
by H.P. Gentileschi
D

Elephant's Easter Eggs
by H.P. Gentileschi
E

Is This a Fish?
by H.P. Gentileschi
F

Gorillas Like Gum
by H.P. Gentileschi
G

THIS HAND
by H.P. Gentileschi
H

INSECTS in my ICE-CREAM
by H.P. Gentileschi
I

When Do You Drink Juice?
by H.P. Gentileschi
J

WHERE IS KATE'S KEY?
by H.P. Gentileschi
K

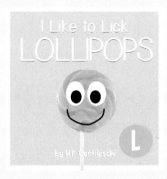

I Like to Lick LOLLIPOPS
by H.P. Gentileschi
L

MILK in My Mailbox
by H.P. Gentileschi
M

DOES A NUT HAVE A NOSE?
by H.P. Gentileschi
N

ONE OCTOPUS in the Olive Tree
by H.P. Gentileschi
O

penguin's paper plane
by H.P. Gentileschi
P

The Queen's Question
by H.P. Gentileschi
Q

Rabbit's Rainbow in Rome
by H.P. Gentileschi
R

Snake's Snacks
by H.P. Gentileschi
S

Does a Tomato Have Teeth?
by H.P. Gentileschi
T

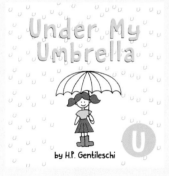

Under My Umbrella
by H.P. Gentileschi
U

Victoria's Violin
by H.P. Gentileschi
V

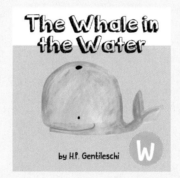

The Whale in the Water
by H.P. Gentileschi
W

Fox Has A Box
by H.P. Gentileschi
X

YOUR YELLOW YO-YO
by H.P. Gentileschi
Y

Zero Zebras in the ZOO!
by H.P. Gentileschi
Z

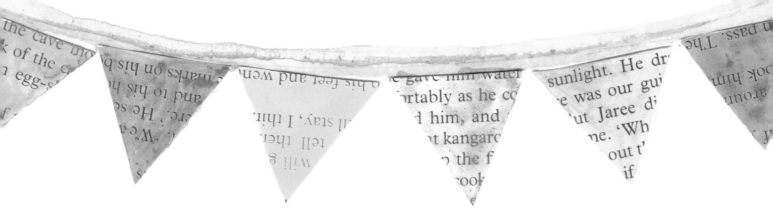

For more engaging activities, teaching resources and to learn more about AlphaBOX books, follow H.P. Gentileschi on:

H.P. Gentileschi

www.hpgentileschi.com

hpgentileschi@gmail.com

We'd love to see how you're using the AlphaBOX series!

Share and tag your photos using:

#alphaboxbooks

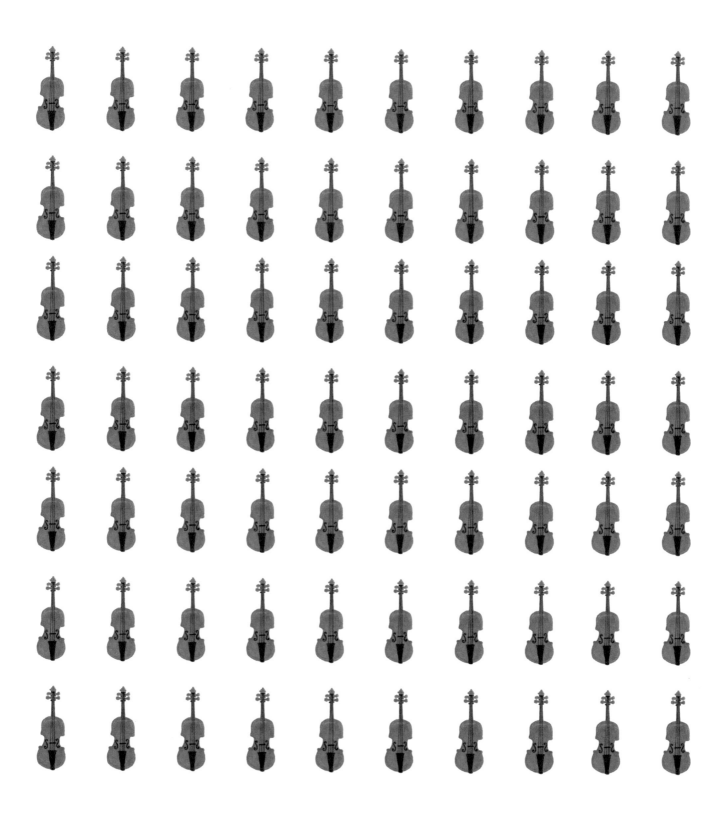